MW01593592

THINGS MY GRANDFATHERS TAUGHT ME

BY RAY D. THROWER

COPYRIGHT NOTICE

FIRST PRINTING 2000 COPIES

ORDER FROM
THOR ENTERPRISES
P.O. BOX 155425
WACO TEXAS 76715

Illustrations by
Vern Herschberger
Trinidad,
Colorado

Printed by
Davis Brothers Publishing Co., Ltd.
Waco, Texas

Dedication

This book is dedicated to my two
grandfathers and grandmothers

King David (aka Horace Dave) Brandon
b. 15 Jan., 1885
d. 7 Feb., 1974

Mary Alma Peltz Brandon
b. 24 Feb., 1885
d. 21 June, 1951

and

Melvin Adam Thrower
b. 8 July, 1884
d. 11 July, 1949

Ada Mae MaGee Thrower
b. 25 Mar., 1886
d. 29 July, 1961

THINGS MY GRANDFATHERS TAUGHT ME

BY

RAY D. THROWER

When I was a young boy and young man, I used to hear my grandfathers and uncles, and other mature men, make wise statements. Many of the statements had a nugget of humor or pathos in them. All seemed to have life's truths bound up in just a few words.

Depending on which direction you came at life, those mature men, sages, always seemed to have a saying to handle it.

I always wondered to myself "Why can't I have those wise thoughts? Why can't I express wise sayings?" Oh, how I would wish.

Maxim 14 was the first that really began to impact me. It is my *maxima propositio.* I finally realized, in my thirties, that my grandfathers and uncles probably hadn't known all these things either, when they were young, and that it had taken them thirty years, after they were kids, to get to the point where I thought they knew everything. They, on the other hand, were likely praying for greater wisdom, realizing how little they knew, as I do now, in my 66th year of life.

I have taken the meaningful sayings of my grandfathers, all my uncles and those older, mature men I've met around the world and combined them into this little book of truths and humor. Adopt a positive attitude toward them. They won't hurt and they might help.

Many of these sayings may have a biblical background. All are in the public domain, in the culture, verbally passed along over the decades and probably the centuries and likely the millennia.

I have recorded the entries in the order I remembered them or as they were given to me.They are grouped, therefore, in a random manner, as they come in life. An index of key words is included at the end of this book to allow rapid location of specific subject matter.

Although the title speaks only of grandfather's teachings, it would be unfair to give total credit to the men. The grandmothers and the aunts would throw in their two bits worth, too, from time to time.

Therefore, let me give them full credit by the following piece of wisdom which I've borrowed and modified. "They also serve who sit and wait...

and stand and cook."

This is by no means a complete work. The variables of life would never allow it to be so. I apologize for it only to the extent that it is based on my own life experiences with whatever limitations or biases that may bring.

I invite you to send me your grandfather's sayings for inclusion in the next edition of this book.

Ray D. Thrower
Waco, Texas 2000 AD

THINGS MY GRANDFATHERS

TAUGHT ME

BY

RAY D. THROWER

1. There's no such thing as a secret.

2. If you never try, you'll never know how close you came to succeeding.

3. Don't make or accept snap judgments.

4. You do marry your mate's family.

5. Men should show as much patience in their relationships with their wives and children as they do when fishing.

6. You can't really appreciate something until you stand back from it for a while.

7. People are like flies on the window pane of life. The ones on the outside want in and the ones on the inside want out.

8. Anger clouds judgment.

9. Alcohol creates the equivalent of anger in the brain. Judgments become clouded.

10. A husband and wife must work as equally yoked oxen or they'll only go in circles and never get anywhere.

11. It only costs a little more to go first class.

12. When you leave a work site, leave as if you're not coming back. Take your tools and other personal items with you.

13. You have to give if you're going to get.

14. It only takes thirty years to become an overnight success.

15. If you can't say something nice about someone, be sure you can run faster than them.

16. Boys will be boys. So will some middle aged men.

17. If you can't handle winter, you don't deserve summer.

18. Bad weather is better than no weather at all.

19. A bad day is better than no day at all.

18. Bad weather is better than no weather at all.

20. Be involved. Don't be in the way.

21. If you don't get what you want, it may be God's way of making room for something bigger and better.

22. The cup of life is always half full, never half empty.

23. A coward dies a lot of times. Brave men die
but once.

24. If you're true to yourself, you can't be untrue to anyone else.

25. Life's too short. It's just that some of the

days are too long.

26. Everybody's going to die someday. You're probably not going to die today.

27. Silence is the best answer to an antagonist.

28. Bloom where you are planted.

29. Never ask anyone to do anything for you that you wouldn't do yourself.

30. A man becomes a man when his father dies.

31. How can I go there when I can't stay here?

32. Sometimes it has to get worse before it gets better.

33. Give up the old ways slowly, cautiously.

34. Act in haste, repent at leisure.

35. There's no defense against criticism except obscurity.

36. When you're dead, it's for a long time.

37. The higher the monkey up the tree, the more of his butt you see.

45. If you want to know how a man will treat his wife, observe how he treats his mother.

38. The need for praise is one of man's deepest needs.

39. Young men think themselves immortal.

40. Procrastination is the thief of time.

41. The tree dies so the violin can sing.

42. You should see the other guy...

43. Every dog has his day.

44. You have to take the bad with the good.

45. If you want to know how a man will treat his wife, observe how he treats his mother.

46. Don't spend all your money in one place.

47. According to Xeno's paradox, the infinite is found in the finite and eternity within a small segment of time.

48. Sex is not the same thing as love.

49. Better a live dog than a dead lion.

50. Better to run away and live to fight another day.

51. If you don't know where you're going any direction will get you there.

52. Love is like building a house. It won't be any good if you don't work at it.

53. It's better to have loved and lost than never to have loved at all.

54. You can take the boy out of the country but you can't take the country out of the boy.

55. As the twig is bent, so grows the tree.

56. You've got to make the ball before you throw it. Did you ever try to throw a piece of string?

57. Better a good friend next door than a

56. Did you ever try to throw a piece of string?

brother far away.

58. All you send into the lives of others comes back into your own.

59. Worry never solved anything.

60. Only the young die innocent.

61. My house, your house.

62. Purveyors of the worst vice always give it at least a small virtue.

63. It's an ill wind that blows no one any good.

64. Fear of the event is worse than the event.

65. After 3 days, company, newspapers and dead fish are all alike.

66. It's never too late to turn over a new leaf.

67. If a son uses bad language, blame the father.

68. The truth shall set you free.

69. Where there's smoke, there's fire.

70 He who laughs last laughs best.

71. Sometimes we have to feast on pride.

72. Treat others the way you want to be treated.

73. To err is human.

74. To blame it on someone else is more human.

75. To forgive is divine.

76. It's lonely at the top.

77. A fool and his money are soon parted.

78. A rational man sees a rational world.

79. A fool lives in a world of confusion.

76. It's lonely at the top.

80. To know a lot, listen a lot, say little.

81. This is the best of all possible worlds.

82. Don't try to keep up with the Joneses.

83. People talk best about themselves.

84. You have to fight fire with fire.

85. You can lead a horse to water but you can't make him drink.

86. Those in charge may not be able to make you do a specific thing but they can make you wish you had done it.

87. Sometimes you have to just raise hell and put a chunk under it.

88. A little knowledge is a dangerous thing.

89. Happiness comes from within.

90. Sometimes you have two chances. Slim and none.

91. It's as plain as the nose on your face.

92. A wise man gets a lot of opinions.

93. Don't stick that bean up your nose.

94. Behind every cloud there's a silver lining.

95. Red sky at night, sailor's delight. Red sky at dawning, sailor take warning.

96. Rome wasn't built in a day.

97. You can't make a silk purse out of a sow's ear.

98. As the old grandparents, aunts and uncles died off, I began to wonder what we'd do without them. Then I realized we were their replacements and the young kids were replacing us.

99. Hell hath no fury like a woman scorned.

99. Hell hath no fury like a woman scorned.

100. Absence makes the heart grow fonder.

101. Actions speak louder than words.

102. Into each life some rain must fall.

103 . Quo Erat Demonstrandum. Q.E.D. The thing speaks for itself.

104. Remember that history is written by the victor.

105. When all else fails, tough it out.

106. Quid Pro Quo. Q.P.Q. This for that. A fair exchange.

107. What you can't cure, you have to endure.

108. Some folks' bark is worse than their bite.

109. May and December are hard to get together.

110. When those who are working for you don't agree with the way you want to do the project, remember it is you, not they, who will have to do the explaining to those above you, if the project goes bad.

111. Forever is a long time.

112. Think before you act.

113. Be content to do one thing and that very well.

114. Once you get something you thought you wanted real bad, it often doesn't seem as important as before.

115. If you think you never make mistakes, you'd better learn to cook. Your first recipe should be crow.

116. A bird in the hand is worth two in the bush.

117. When someone presses for an immediate answer, at least recite the alphabet to yourself be-

118. Bad breath is better than no breath at all.

fore answering.

118. Bad breath is better than no breath at all.

119. The horse and plow are slow but the earth is patient.

120. The slow flow of water will wear the deepest canyon.

121. The truth is hard enough to remember, much less a lie.

122. If I believe God exists and you do not and if there isn't a God, neither of us has lost anything. But, if I believe and you don't and there is a God, you've lost everything.

123. Q. How are you?
A. Pretty good for an old guy.
Q. You don't look so old!
A. Well, I've lived a sheltered life.
[Use this only if you're over 60 and have *not* lived a sheltered life]

124. Remember that God lets us be young so we can make mistakes when people expect us to.

125. Learn from the mistakes of others.

126. Sometimes the dragon loses.

127. Be the anvil, not the hammer. The anvil wears out the hammers, you know.

128. Time wounds all heels.

129. Wisdom is gained more by change in attitude than passage of time.

130. It's not enough to feed the body. You must also feed the soul.

131. If you want the rainbow, accept the rain.

132. Never remind others of the good thing you've done for them.

133. As we age, we change many attitudes, so, we shouldn't be too judgmental when young. Nei-

136. Lie down with dogs, get up ewith fleas.

ther should we judge the young too harshly when we're old.

134. Nothing succeeds like success.

135. Some folks are closer than the hands of a clock at five minutes to eleven.

136. Lie down with dogs, get up with fleas.

137. It's better to remain silent and have people *think* you're a fool than to speak and remove all doubt.

138. Patience wins all battles.

139. Let the hide go with the tallow.

140. All you step on, on the way up the ladder of success, you'll meet again on the way down.

141. If you don't change directions you'll wind up where you're going.

142. There's always somebody worse off.

143. Be reasonable. Do it my way.

144. The Ark was built by beginners. The Titanic was built by professionals.

145. If you're good to mine, you're good to me.

146. If the shoe fits, wear it.

147. The past is water under the bridge and sand over the desert.

148. If you fail to remember and consider the past you are likely to repeat it.

149. A promise is a promise.

150. Time is the most difficult thing to kill.

151. Some men are iron marshmallows.

152. Don't bite the hand that feeds you.

150. Time is the most difficult thing to kill.

153. Early to bed and early to rise makes one healthy, wealthy and wise.

154. If confusion begins in a social or business environment, look for a catalyst, usually a person.

155. When loading anything, load biggest first, heaviest lowest. Nest smaller, lighter items around larger, heavier items.

156. Except for written exams, when you have a number of tasks to perform, first:

a. do the most difficult
b. do the furthest away
c. do the one requiring the most time (except

for written exams).

Save for last:

a. the easy ones (except for written exams).
b. the closest.
c. the one requiring the least time.

157. Don't worry about people who make errors. They're doing something. Worry about those who appear not to make mistakes.

158. The buck stops here.

159. Time is the great equalizer of us all.

160. Win a few, lose a few.

161. If at first you don't succeed, try, try again.

162. Don't be selfish.

163. Don't pray to God for patience. He might give it to you and you might have to use it.

164. Genius is supposed to be high intellect but it's really just a stubborn, unwilling to quit, attitude.

165. It's not attaining the goal but overcoming the obstacles to the goal that matters.

166. It's better to have failed while trying, than never to have tried at all.

171. If it looks like a duck and quacks like a duck and waddles like a duck, it's probably a duck.

167. Reach up to God as far as you can and he'll reach down the rest of the way.

168. Keep calm.

169. Most people marvel at the human hand with its opposing thumb. I marvel at how the hand perfectly fits the human forehead when we realize we've made a mistake. Oh, No!

170. Straight arrows don't fly backwards. Ever.

171. If it looks like a duck and quacks like a duck and waddles like a duck, it's probably a duck.

172. You carry boredom with you. Lose the

baggage.

173. We become a part of what we condone.

174. Boredom is an attitude of self, not others.

175. If you live in a glass house don't throw stones.

176. If you're penny wise don't be pound foolish.

177. Don't cry over spilled milk.

178. When the damage is done, when trouble is over, go on to bigger and better things.

179. Tempus Fugit. Time Flies.

180. The bigger they come, the harder they fall.

181. He who sits highest, falls furthest.

182. Men are often bound by chains they forge themselves.

183. One enemy is too many.

184. Don't judge other people. Maybe God's not through with them yet.

185. You can't shelter folks 24 hours a day. If

182. Men are often bound by chains they forge themselves.

they're going to get in trouble, they'll find a way.

186. Have simple tastes and that only the best.

187. Never say "never". Well, hardly ever.

188. One true loving hug is better than 1000 casual sexual encounters.

189. If you know you've got enough, you're truly wealthy.

190. The first mark of wisdom. Don't start an argument.

191. Life isn't always what we want and what we

get isn't always as bad as we think.

192. One hundred years from now it won't make any difference so be happy now.

193. Prayers, unlike songs, don't always require words.

194. If you've never worked, you really can't enjoy resting.

195. A wink's as good as a nod and a prayer, whispered, not shouted, to God.

196. Be sure you know another man's standards before you agree to them.

197. Look before you leap.

198. The more difficult the struggle, the sweeter the victory.

199. Never *promise,* in advance, to do something unless you know what it is and actually agree to it.

200. It's better to forget and smile than remember and be sad.

201. Parents love their children immediately as they're born but it takes the passage of time for children to learn to love their parents.

197. Look before you leap.

202. If it ain't broke, don't fix it!

203. I spent six months in a rough place one night.

204. The early bird gets the worm.

205. Opinions are like noses. Everybody is entitled to at least one.

206. There's no honor in being poor. But, there's no great shame, either.

207. If you *think* God's trying to tell you something, listen a little harder.

208. You can't take it with you.

209. Our mountains and plains don't need our trash.

210. All work and no play makes Jack.

211. Share and share alike.

212. If you're going to be a high profile figure, also figure on being a target.

213. The earth is 7/8th's water and 1/8th land. Obviously, God meant for man to go fishing seven times as much as he meant for us to work.

214. No one is ever hurt by abstinence.

215. You have to melt the brass and pour and form it before you can hear the sweetness of music from the horn.

216. Abstinence is the best birth control method. It's also the most ethical.

217. A friend, in time of need, is a friend, indeed.

218. Life isn't always what we want.

219. Those who can keep their heads when all around them are losing theirs just don't understand the situation.

212. If you're going to be a high profile figure, also figure on being a target.

220. You can't go forward by looking back.

221. If the camel gets its nose under the edge of the tent the rest of the body is sure to follow.

222. You can't fly on one wing.

223. Life is a variable. Don't get upset if it varies.

224. When you have a tiger by the tail, it's too late to let go.

225. Sleep as if you're in the arms of Morpheus.

226. If it works, don't fix it.

227. He who will not risk will not win..

228. Nothing lasts forever.

229. The best is yet to come.

230. If your mother ever calls you by all of your names, you can be sure of one thing. You're in trouble.

231. If you plant thistles you sure won't grow roses.

232. Some people make light of everything. It's their way of coping with heavy issues. Accept them.

233. Respect is earned.

234. Success is 1% inspiration and 99% perspiration.

235. Don't rock the boat when you're in it.

236. Nature abhors a vacuum.

237. It's better to be a willing contributor than a beneficiary.

238. Anticipation of the event is greater than the event.

231. If you plant thistles you sure won't grow roses.

239. Man's greatest work is honest praise to God.

240. Laugh and the world laughs with you. Weep and you weep alone.

241. A man's word is his bond.

242. Take the bull by the horns.

243. Not making a decision is making a decision, too.

244. If it sounds too good to be true, it probably is.

245. The way to a man's heart is by his stomach.

246. Question almost everything. Accept God on faith.

247. A man is actually three men. The man he thinks he is, the man others see him as and the man he really is.

248. Never compromise your ethics.

249. If you feel something is wrong, it probably is. Don't do it.

250. Keep your mind active. You'll live longer.

251. It's better to stand apart and watch the crowd than it is to mill around as part of the crowd.

252. Never say die.

253. There's more than one way to skin a cat.

254. Many people have problems now because they didn't make decisions about the future in the past.

255. You've got to have the rain if you're going to have the flowers.

256. If you have two loaves of bread, sell one and buy some flowers for the table so you can feed

259. Laughter really is the best medicine.

not only the body but the soul.

257. Be cautious of fair weather friends.

258. Better a good friend nearby than a brother far away.

259. Laughter really is the best medicine.

260. Don't allow yourself to be an educated fool.

261. Study the theory but get your hands dirty so you can really understand.

262. Things work better, sometimes, when you do them opposite to what appears best. Peel the envelope from the stamp, not the stamp from the

envelope.

263. A friend is one who takes the wheat and chaff of our lives and, with the breath of understanding love, blows the chaff away.

264. Sometimes you have to ignore the messenger in order to hear the message.

265. You don't have to fix my trouble. Just listen.

266. The most useless things are a dull knife and an unloaded gun.

267. If someone is antagonizing you, keep your head on your shoulders and your fist in your pocket.

268. Necessity is the mother of invention.

269. Find a need and fill it.

270. The truth will set you free. It won't always make you happy.

271. Life is good if one is still learning.

272. Luck comes mostly from hard work.

273. Measure twice, cut once.

279. You can't please everybody.

274. Enough is as good as a feast.

275. Flattery is like soap. Mostly lye.

276. It's not over 'till it's over.

277. Once you take your hand from the pawn, you've made your play.

278. To really be attentive...Listen to what's *not* being said.

279. You can't please everybody.

280. A job, once begun, isn't finished until it's done.

281. Shoot low, Pete. He's riding a Shetland.

282. The bell that's been rung cannot be unrung.

283. Placing blame is unproductive.

284. Pay attention to those still small voices.

285. Making mistakes is part of life's learning process.

286. All things, good and bad, have a beginning and an end.

287. Blame it on the weather.

288. Don't count your chickens before they hatch.

289. Neither borrower nor lender be.

290. Save your money first, then pay cash. Don't finance anything.

291. The IRS is not your friend.

292. Some folks are like a block of ten year old concrete. Mixed up and well set.

293. Make a decision.

294. Don't vacillate.

300. Never try to teach a pig to sing. You'll get frustrated and you'll make the pig mad.

295. Every dog has his day.

296. Today is the first day of the rest of your life.

297. Just a word, to the wise, should be sufficient.

298. Some folks are slow as the seven year itch.

299. It takes two to make a bargain.

300. Never try to teach a pig to sing. You'll get frustrated and you'll make the pig mad.

301. The eyes are the gateway to the soul.

302. Do it when you think about it.

303. You can't miss something you never had.

304. He who toots not his own horn, the same shall not be tooted.

305. Enjoy giving without thinking of receiving
.

306. Opportunity knocks only once.

307. It would be a dull world if we all agreed on everything.

308. There's an opportunity hidden in every obstacle.

309. If life were simple, it would be boring.

310. You become what you read.

311. Children are the future. Treat them well.

312. When I work, I work hard. When I think, I fall asleep.

313. Change can be uncomfortable if you are not prepared for it.

314. Rank has its privileges.

315. Remember the cardinal virtues. Prudence,

320. Never cry wolf if there's no wolf.

temperance, fortitude and justice.

316. The tree that has no winds to buffet it will not develop a strong root system and will fall when a real storm comes. People need buffeting, too.

317. When you are a high profile person, expect to be shot at even by members of your family.

318. A stitch in time saves nine.

319. You can't make a silk purse out of a sow's ear. But, you can tan it and make a neat coin purse.

320. Never cry wolf if there's no wolf.

321. There are two sides to every story and then there's the story.

322. Within each of us is the key to success.

323. If you're where you want to be and doing what you want to do, that's all that matters.

324. You have to put the past behind you before you can go forward.

325. Don't make decisions in anger.

326. It really isn't love until you give it away, unconditionally.

327. If it's stupid and it works, it isn't stupid.

328. A place to go is home. Someone to love is family. Having both is a blessing.

329. Always speak encouraging words.

330. If you learn to read well you can learn to do anything.

331. If there are unexpected delays, just consider it as an extension to a pleasant experience.

332. If the dog hadn't stopped to scratch he would have caught the rabbit.

338. Never pee into the wind.

333. If you have to ask "Can I afford it", you probably can't.

334. Necessity never made a good bargain

335. If you have to ask "Can I afford it?", be sure to ask "Can I not afford it?".

336. God couldn't be everywhere at once. That's why he made mothers.

337. Not doing something for fear you'll fail assures failure.

338. Never pee into the wind.

339. Don't get mad, get even.

340. The road to hell is paved with good intentions.

341. If I'd known I was going to live this long, I'd have taken better care of myself.

342. The true measure of a person is what he does when no one is around.

343. Blood is thicker than water.

344. Smile. Make people wonder what you've been up to.

345. If you got along without it this long you can get along without it a while longer.

346. Never drive your motorcycle behind a cattle truck.

347. Business dealings with family are risky. There's a psychological factor involved. So don't.

348. If a man does the best he can but still can't be successful, don't find fault with him.

349 When you're in a hole, grab a shovel and dig your way out.

350. Love is like a knot. It takes two to tie one.

346. Never drive your motorcycle behind a cattle truck.

351. If you place a small value on yourself, the world will not raise the price.

352. Most successful businessmen have some failures behind them.

353. Take care of today. Let tomorrow take care of itself.

354. If you can't trust the messenger, how can you trust the message?

355. When all else fails, read the instructions.

356. Manners are how we display our morals.

357. If you're bad to others and something bad happens to you, no one will care.

358. Self discipline is learned in the face of adversity.

359. If you try to get too much, you may wind up with nothing at all.

360. You'll catch more flies with sugar than with vinegar.

361. Look before you leap and think twice before you act.

362. Memories are what we build when we're young and what we have when we're old, so build good, happy ones.

363. Every action in the presence of others should show some respect to those present.

364. We need people who are willing to throw tea in the harbor once in a while.

365. It is better to be alone than in bad company.

366. Don't be sneaky in your manner.

367. Every man is his own ruler.

368. For everything there is a season.

364. We need people who are willing to throw tea in the harbor once in a while.

369. Compassion is feeling another person's anguish or pain.

370. Talk is cheap. Everybody wants to talk. Nobody wants to listen.

371. It's not a perfect world. But, it'll do until one comes around.

372. Make hay while the sun shines.

373. If momma ain't happy, ain't nobody happy.

374. The road to a friend's house is never long.

375. If you love something, let it go. If it comes

back, it's yours. If it doesn't, it never was.

376. Our loyalties are indicators of the kind of person we are to become.

377. Truth never dies.

378. The candle which lights another candle loses none of its light.

379. Slow and steady win the race.

380. Doing what is right takes moral courage.

381. Anything worth having is worth waiting for.

382. A difference of opinion is not necessarily a difference in ethics.

383. Don't be critical of another unless you've walked in their shoes for a month.

384. If someone asks if you have "checked it" and you have checked it, check it again, anyway.

385. There will always be those who won't like you if you succeed.

386. If you don't work from within for change, you have no right to complain.

387. When you do something good, rarely will

392. If anything goes wrong, you can always blame it on the dog.

anyone be around to see it. Do it anyway.

388. When you make a mistake, the bigger it is the more people will be around to observe.

389. You can do everything perfectly for an entire year, 8760 hours, but make a one minute mistake and that's what people will remember you for.

390. It's not wrong to have wealth. No one would have remembered the good Samaritan if he'd only had good intentions.

391. Restraint and liberty are equals.

392. If anything goes wrong, you can always

blame it on the dog.

393. It does no good to beat a dead horse.

394. Opposites attract but oil and water won't mix.

395. Learn to disagree but don't be disagreeable.

396 A good friend is a blessing but each of us must be his own Rock of Gibraltar.

397. I was looking for a job when I found this one.

398. If you're going to do something important, do it like you'd remove a Bandaid ®. Quickly.

399. There's no such thing as a free lunch.

400. As fathers, we've taught our sons about all we can by the time they're in their teens. It's up to them to learn when to apply that knowledge.

401. Be quick to praise. Be slow to criticize.

402 Know your subject well before speaking.

403. There's no gain without a little pain.

404. The customer may not always be right but he's always the customer.

**409. If you don't vote
you have no right to complain.**

405. When the student is ready to learn the teacher will appear.

406. Love is the one thing you can give away and never run out of.

407. Lead or follow but get out of the way.

408. Carpe Diem. Seize the day. Grab the opportunity.

409. If you don't vote, you have no right to complain.

410. The boss may not always be right but he's always the boss.

411. Always be aware of your surroundings. Be conscious of what's going on.

412. Don't block the way of others.

413. When the boss is wrong, see number 410.

414. Coarse language shows lack of personal discipline.

415. One swallow doesn't make a spring.

416. Many people spend the first half of their lives afraid of life and the second half fearing death. Enjoy both halves.

417. Easy come, easy go.

418. Never sign a blank form.

419. The less you tell about what you're doing, the less you have to explain if it goes wrong.

420. Sometimes there just is no answer to "Why".

421. Turn about is fair play.

422. It's not what you know, it's knowing how to find out.

423. Faith attacked is faith defended.

414. Coarse language shows lack of personal discipline.

424. Don't worry so much about learning as understanding.

425. Men should make laws which do not require men to kneel to the laws or the lawmakers.

426. Lawmakers should have to live by the laws they pass.

427. Wherever you go, there you are.

428. Some parts of life can be a long fight with a short stick.

429. Truth remains constant. Man's perception or application of truth varies.

430. You never know it's too late until it's too late.

431. Birds of a feather flock together. Be careful who you hang out with.

432. One event is not a trend.

433. All men are created equal. Some are just more equal than others.

434. Sometimes to wait is best.

435. If you become prosperous, be sure to temper it with taste and quiet generosity.

436. The greater the risk, the greater the return.

437. If you think you've got it bad read the Book of Job.

438. If you're going to take credit for the rain be ready to take the blame for the drought.

439. Right makes might.

440. Hold fast to your integrity. Don't let others talk you into doing something morally wrong.

441. A deal is a deal.

442. Be sure you are persevering and not just be-

447. Try lighting a single charcoal briquette. Try lighting a bunch of them piled together. Likewise, people come together for spiritual guidance for the same reason.

ing plain old stubborn.

443. Thin may be in but fat's where it's at.

444. Never make a threat. Make a promise.

445. All men are the same, as individuals. It's politics and leadership which make them different.

446. Hold fast to that which is right and good.

447. Try lighting a single charcoal briquette. Try lighting a bunch of them piled together. Likewise, people come together for spiritual guidance for the same reason.

448. All good ideas have something simple as their foundation.

449. Look at your obstacles as a tool to get to the goal the obstacle is blocking.

450. Make do the best you can with what you have.

451. There's safety in numbers.

452. Perseverance can overcome a lack of inherent ability.

453. Nudge the tiller of life. Not big changes. Just little ones.

454. We only live once. Or, do we?

455. Food is the center of the universe.

456. Cream will always rise to the top.

457. You can't have it both ways

458. All beginnings are with limited knowledge.

459. In life, as in sailing, we don't know which way the wind will blow when we begin, so we tack.

460. In the final analysis, when the score is

464. No husband has ever been shot while doing dishes.

counted, apathy rules.

461. He that knows that he knows not, and acknowledges not that he knows not, is a fool.

462. He that knows that he knows not and acknowledges that he knows not is wise. Teach him.

463. If you don't like what you're doing, don't do it.

464. No husband has ever been shot while doing the dishes.

465. If you can't handle the hard times, you don't deserve the good times.

466. In brainstorming sessions, never, ever put down the other guy or his ideas.

467. Don't just stand there, do something.
468. If someone else does it, you can't take the credit.

469. Do something, even if it's wrong.

470. It's easier to do it right than to do it over.

471. True worth is in being, not seeming to be.

472. Left to our own devices, we tend to move toward chaos.

473. Some answers are pretty dumb.

474. Every problem is really an opportunity.

475. If you can't get what you want or need, don't get frustrated. Just do the best you can with what you have.

476. A fine is a tax for doing bad. A tax is a fine for doing well.

477. The power to tax is the power to destroy.

478. If we fail to pass along specific standards of right and wrong we must share the blame for future

474. Every problem is really an opportunity.

failings in character.

479. There are some things we are just not meant to know.

480. There are some things we don't need to know.

481. Some things we don't want to know.

482. Don't worry so much about knowing as understanding. Understand all you know.

483. Whatever you do, do with all your energy.

484. You can get cheaper oats. But, they've usually been through the horse once.

485. Problems are seldom as bad as we think they'll be. Likewise, our fantasies and dreams, in reality, are seldom as exotic as we think they'll be.

486. Don't wish for something at a level of desperation. Always be willing to do without.

487. Don't be judgmental. You probably don't know the whole story, certainly not both sides.

488. Try not to tell your side of the story with a skew. Seek an even balance.

489. If I'd wanted home cookin' I'd of stayed at home.

490. Always ask , "Is winning worth the price?".

491. It's not things or events which help make you happy but good relationships.

492. It's better to do it right than to do it over.

493. Sometimes it's best to yield. Even the biggest tree bends when beat by heavy winds.

494. When intellect is pitted against superstition, superstition wins almost everytime.

495. Often, it's easier to get forgiveness than it is to get permission.

370. Never dip your pen in the company ink.

496. I cannot show you God just as I cannot show you the wind. But, I can show you the works of God just as I can show you the works of the wind.

497. If ten thousand people say a stupid thing, it doesn't make it right. It is still stupid.

498. Hatred destroys the one who hates.

499. Never dip your pen in the company ink

500. If you always do what you've always done, you'll always get what you always got.

501. If someone copies what you do or say, re-

member, mimicking is the sincerest form of flattery.

502. Despise the sin, not the sinner.

503. When two lives come together, no matter how briefly, they can never be totally separated.

504. The relative numerical value of verbal quantities runs about like this:

All	100%
Most	80%
Many	65%
A lot	50%
Some	35%
A few	20%
None	0%

The relationship of opposites is:

All - None
Most - A Few
Many - Some

505. We learn more from our mistakes and failures than we do from our successes and victories.

506. When you quit learning you quit living.

507. Just remember, when *trying* to do something, a steer can *try*.

509. The pen is mightier than the sword.

508. Persistence should be directed toward worthwhile goals.

509. The pen is mightier than the sword.

510. There are three ways to do important things.The right way, the wrong way or the Government way.

511. Never complain about how hard your job is. A lot of other people would do it at a less pay.

512. Don't you ever wonder what politicians have on each other that they'll compromise themselves for one another?

513. Be grateful government is inefficient. We sure don't want all the government we pay for.

514. In choosing a mate, a horse, or a car, a person must please one's self and not attend to the opinions and advice of friends, relatives or associates.

515. Stick with me and see what the next 50 years brings.

516. A busy person hasn't time to worry.

517. There are no dumb questions.

518. Have patience with those who lack understanding.

519. He who is short with those who ask, so as to learn, is himself lacking in knowledge and grace.

520. The first dollar often is harder to earn than the second million.

521. If you don't explore the limits of your rights, they will become limited by others.

522. Do the hard things of life while they're easy to do.

523. The correct tool gets things done, in labor

523. The correct tool gets things done, in labor or in dealing with people. You can't shovel water.

or in dealing with people. You can't shovel water.

524. A smart quip proves nothing.

525. It takes a lot of bread to toast the town.

526. An ounce of mother's love is worth a ton of priestly concern.

527. If your job was easy, everybody would be doing it.

528. If a guy often goes TOO FAR out of his way for another, ask what the other has on the one. Avoid both until you know more.

529. No matter how hard you polish on it, you can't polish crap.

530. You appreciate things more if you work for them.

531. You conserve things more if you have to pay for them.

532. No, Rome wasn't built in a day, but then I wasn't in charge.

533. If Christianity were a sham it could not have lasted 200 years, let alone almost 2,000.

534. Never squat when you're wearing your spurs.

535. You can be in total control. Just remember if it flops, you're totally at fault.

536. Carry a little notebook and note things you don't want to forget. Transcribe the notes later to a day journal. Make this a lifelong habit.

537. Sometimes, to do nothing is best.

538. Respect the privacy and property of others.

539. To be a good conversationalist, listen.

540. Just as the apple doesn't fall far from the

543. If at all possible, don't make major decisions at night. Wait till broad daylight.

apple tree, people tend be like their families.

541. A good way to cure the blues is to do something nice for someone else.

542. Unreasonable folks rarely change. Stay away from them.

543. If at all possible, don't make major decisions at night. Wait till broad daylight.

544. Be the trailblazer not the trail follower.

545. Read a book each week on a subject new to you.

546. If you worry and are lonesome and think you aren't cared for, volunteer to work for a while in a retirement home or hospital.

547. If you can't stand the heat, stay out of the kitchen.

548. It's not what you have but what you are that matters.

549. Be especially kind with old people. You'll be there some day.

550. If you make a mistake, admit it. It'll defuse criticism and you can go on to better things.

551. You can please all the people some of the time and some of the people all the time but never all the people all the time.

552. Yes, hang up your clothes and fold your underwear. It's easier to find and keeps longer. And you'll know what's clean and what isn't.

553. Always be open to new knowledge, a new language, archaeology, geography, medicine, math, history, physics, chemistry, religion, music, astronomy, pottery, writing, etc. Select a group and study it intensely for a year.

554. Marriage is a two way proposition. Both parties have to compromise so both can be happy.

559. Work without dispute,
It's the only way life is tolerable.

555. It's fun to do jig saw puzzles in the mind and invent the parts as you go along, based on new incoming data.

556. Make the best of an imperfect world because once in a while imperfection will surround you.

557. It's far better to try something and fail than to take rank with those legions who have never tried at all.

558. Every successful person has a list of failures before the success.

559. Work without dispute, It's the only way

life is tolerable.

560. Some people have tact. Other people tell the truth.

561. Integrity has to overrule tact.

562. He who gives, lives.

563. If you know, don't blab.

564. If you want to win, have patience.

565. He who wins, has patience.

566. A friend who borrows from you often is not a friend.

567. Never do what you wouldn't want others to know.

568. It is better to try, and fail, than never try at all, which assures failure.

569. A committee is a group which keeps minutes and loses hours.

570. It can get beat up, rained on, smudged, bent and dented but it'll always be a Stetson. Quality always tells. In anything.

571. Life is not getting and having but being and

574. When you're working out of a vehicle, with papers, never open two doors at the same time.

becoming.

572. It's not what you have but what you do with what you have.

573. Sometimes life just jumps up, slaps you in the face and says "you're not paying attention!". Pay attention.

574. When you're working out of a vehicle, with papers, never open two doors at the same time.

575. When you part ways, always have a positive point of contact for the future.

576. If you agree to work for a price, do it for

what you agreed to even if you find that someone else got more, later on, for less work.

577. Always put back something for a rainy day. You never know when you might have to move your tent to another village.

578. When traveling across the desert make sure your camel never vapor locks.

579. Always use the right tool for the right job. Just remember that if God wants a hammer to do the work of a screwdriver, it will do very well, thank you.

580. Keep your word.

581. Be wary of those who talk about you behind your back before your very eyes.

582. Don't carry over grudges from the past of others.

583. Whether Democrat or Republican, be American first.

584. "Close" counts only in horseshoes, hand grenades and atomic bombs.

585. Don't justify yourself by condemning others.

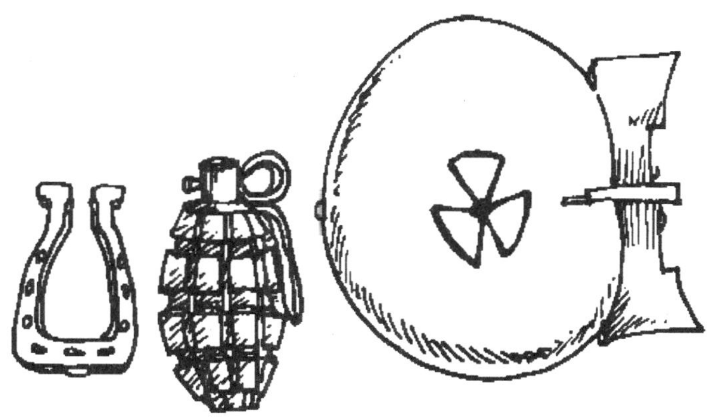

584.“Close” counts only in horseshoes, hand grenades and atomic bombs.

586. You can fight city hall.

587. Right makes might.

588. If you fight and run away, you’ll live to fight another day.

589. If you know, don’t blab. If you guess, don’t gab.

590. It takes ten “attaboys” to make up for one “I gotcha”.

591. You have to study a situation to know when it’s time and then you’ll often miss the mark.

592. Time waits for no one.

593. Timing often is everything.

594. Our forefathers built a mighty nation without taking coffee breaks.

595. If you watch your mouth you'll stay out of trouble.

596. While waiting for your ship to come in remember that it'll sail better on smooth seas. Don't make waves.

597. The secret to sweet success is the salty sweat of your brow.

598. Self control is better than self expression.

599. You can't command until you know how to obey.

600. A turtle has to stick its neck out if it is going to make progress. Be like the turtle.

601. Don't marry for money. It's cheaper to just get a loan.

602. If you make a mistake it proves you at least tried.

603. A man can't send another man flowers. But

600. A turtle has to stick its neck out if it is going to make progress. Be like the turtle.

a man can send another man a cactus.

604. Life is like a cactus in bloom. You can't have the beauty without the thorns and if you handle the cactus correctly you'll never feel the thorns. Just like life.

605. Watching the errors of other folks, you should be able to avoid making all of them yourself.

606. If we learn obedience we learn to lead.

607. The less you do today the more you have to do tomorrow.

608. If you raise roses or other flowers in your garden, your neighbors can enjoy them too.

609. Even a little lie is bad. It weakens the soul.

610. Give a man a fish and he can feed himself for a day. Teach a man to fish and he can feed himself and others for a lifetime.

611. The key to being a good conversationalist is being a good listener.

612. True happiness exists when shared with another.

613. If a rabbit's foot is so lucky, how'd the rabbit lose his?

614. A mistake is not a loss if one gains experience.

615. Courage can turn a single man into a majority.

616. You can't be fit as a fiddle when you're tight as a drum.

617. Never do anything that can't be undone, like tattoos. You may change. It won't.

618. Haste doesn't substitute for action.

617. Never do anything that can't be undone, like tattoos. You may change. It won't.

619. He who tells the absolute truth must always have one foot in the stirrup.

620. Be cautious about making excuses for someone else. You may not know all the details. The same with blame.

621. Are you blessed? Remember, God blesses us so others can be blessed through us.

622. Don't cross your bridges till you come to them.

623. Remember that the bridges you cross before you get to them are over rivers that probably don't exist.

624. There's a lot of difference between doing something and understanding why it should be done.

625. Being there is a lot different than getting there.

626. God made tomorrow so we don't have to do everything today.

627. It is better to have self control than to control legions.

628. Sometimes it's not good enough to do your best. You have to do what is required.

629. Quality never needs justification.

630. A person who can laugh at himself will have
laughter for a lifetime.

631. Live your life so that when you die the mourners outnumber the cheering section.

632. Make your wife or girl friend feel better by asking "How was heaven when you left?".

633. Don't ever try to build yourself up by tearing someone else down.

634. The rooster thinks he's important but remember, the sun doesn't rise to hear him crow.

634. The rooster thinks he's important but remember, the sun doesn't rise to hear him crow.

635. Better an old hat than a bare head.

636. God never takes one thing away but something else is given.

637. If you have to climb a hill, waiting around won't make it smaller.

638. Turn your obstacles into opportunities.

639. Wealth doesn't create happiness but it does provide for a pleasant sort of misery.

640. Reputation and character differ in that reputation can be made or lost in a moment whereas character takes a lifetime to build.

641. Some scientists say there is no God, that life began when a lightning bolt hit some molecules in the ancient seas. But, who made the lightning bolt, the molecules and the ancient seas?

642. People are like little swatches of cloth. One little swatch won't keep your nose warm on a cold day. But, bind them together with a common bond and they make a quilt which is more valuable than the sum of all the parts. So it is with faith.

643. While you brag about how fast you are someone else might run past you. Don't brag.

644. It's a small world but I'd hate to have to paint it.

645. Live so that when others remember you they think of fairness, honesty and integrity.

646. Anger begets anger. Stay calm.

647. It's better to be cheated once in a while than to live always being suspicious.

648. The easiest thing to lose is trust.

649. The hardest thing to regain is trust.

650. When a man gives his word, he becomes responsible.

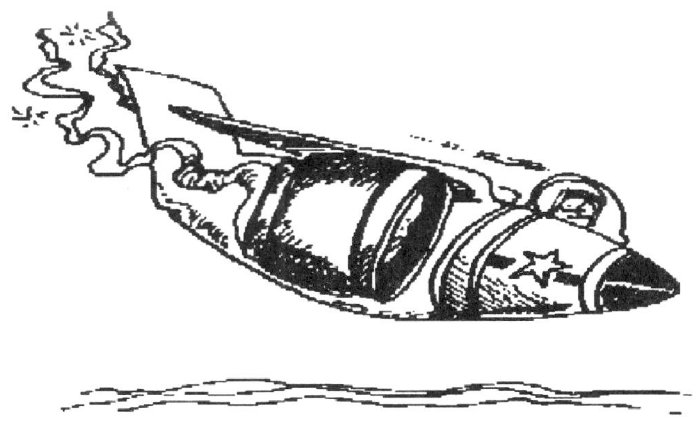

652. If you're making a low level flight over the desert, be sure your air filters are capable of passing air and blocking sand for the entire flight.

651. You have to like yourself before others can like you.

652. If you're making a low level flight over the desert, be sure your air filters are capable of passing air and blocking sand for the entire flight.

653. Let your glass always be half full, not half empty, the road pavement always starting, not ending, your garden getting ready for next spring, not dying this winter, life beginning, not ending.

654. Think positive. Turn it over to God if you can't handle it.

655. It's harder to get out of trouble than it is to get in trouble.

656. Not making a choice is making a choice.

657. If you have a difficult job, break it into small components. They'll be easier to handle.

658. It's hard to be wise and patient when you're starving.

659. Plan a job before you do it. It'll go easier.

660. Nobody really dies until he's forgotten.

661. If you always remember a woman's birthday but never her age, you'll be ready for the diplomatic corps.

662. The world is full of willing people. Some willing to work and others willing to let them.

663. Taxation without representation is tyranny. Taxation with representation's not so good either.

664. Youth is the best time to be poor.

665. Just because something is obscure doesn't mean it's profound.

666. Just because something is easy to understand doesn't mean it isn't profound.

667. Truth is its own reward.

596. Nobody would have blamed Columbus if he'd turned back. Nobody would remember him, either.

668. Never discuss important things where you cannot see who is listening.

669. Never discuss important things with those who are not involved.

670. Never smoke upwind of people who don't like it.

671. If you're last in the chow line, everyone else will be through, you'll still be eating and you'll seldom have to do the dishes.

672. Nobody would have blamed Columbus if he'd turned back. Nobody would remember him, either.

673. Sleep, riches and health must be interrupted

to be fully appreciated.

674. When you start to criticize others, remember, they haven't had all your advantages.

675. Reserving judgment is a measure of infinite love.

676. Even plants need a little shadow to grow well. So it is with our lives.

677. A true leader is like a shepherd. He goes ahead of and behind the flock, wherever needed.

678. If you're sure where you're going the world will move aside.

679. A man who burns his candle at both ends winds up with a short wick.

680. The lazy find poverty in old age, the diligent find a harvest of plenty.

681. The gift may be light as a feather but the meaning as heavy as a mountain.

682. It's not how much time you put in but what you do with the time you put in.

683. All things being equal, the simplest answer is usually the correct one.

688. The longest journey begins with a single step.

684. If you can't handle the tough times, do you deserve the good times?

685. Anything worth doing is worth doing.

686. A wise man is one who discovers what he does best, according to his God given skills and abilities, and does it.

687. If the buzzards are circling, you're working too slow.

688. The longest journey begins with a single step.

689. You can't hold much with a balled up fist but you can hold much with a gentle, open palm.

690. Justice is temporary. Conscience is forever.

691. A small house holds as much happiness as a big house.

692. Life is uncertain at best. Eat dessert first.

693. A truly wise man always has more questions than answers.

694. It takes less time to do it right than explain why you didn't.

695. Sure you can trust the government. Just ask the Indians.

696. The early bird gets the worm but the second mouse gets the cheese.

697. When you say "I can't", it usually means "I don't want to".

698. Not everything can be fully resolved.

699. Children keep secrets better than adults.

700. If you pray, don't worry. If you worry, pray instead.

701. If you don't change directions, you'll wind up where you're going.

707. It's hard to soar with eagles when you hang out with turkeys.

702. Always be prepared to walk away if it doesn't feel right.

703. Think before you speak. You can't be hurt by what you don't say. You can't hurt others, either.

704. Problems are opportunities in disguise.

705. Unless you prepare to win you are preparing to fail.

706. It's hard to soar with eagles when you hang out with turkeys.

707. The best thing a father can do for his kids is to love their mother. Vice versa.

708. Stumbling blocks or stepping stones. They're all the same. It's just how you use them.

709. The opposite of faith is fear.

710. Understand others so as to like them.

711. You can be effective if you're committed.

712. Sometimes you have to ask yourself, "What am I doing here?".

713. Some battles aren't worth fighting.

714. It's not enough to just believe in God. So did the demons.

715. "We have come of age" is an arrogant expression.

716. It's all in how you look at things. Even a cow pie is a picnic to a fly.

717. When you marry a mountain woman, you don't just marry the woman, you marry the entire mountain, too.

718. When speaking before a group, don't apologize for something that you forgot. They likely won't think of it as missing if you don't tell them.

719. Haste is Satan's most trusted companion.

716. It's all in how you look at things. Even a cow pie is a picnic to a fly.

720. Be deliberate in all your judgments.

721. Panic is never an appropriate response.

722. Example is better than advice.

723. To err is human. To really foul things up requires a computer.

724. An empty wagon makes more noise than a full wagon. People, too.

725. It's better to fail with a plan than to succeed without a plan.

726. You get into more trouble defending the

mistake than making the mistake.

727. God forgave King David, why not you?

728. Finders keepers, losers weepers. If the owner is identifiable, return it to them. If they are not identifiable, it's yours. It doesn't belong to the police.

729. The difficulties of peace are better than the agonies of war.

730. You may not be where you want to be or where you're going to be but you're not where you were.

731. Experiences of the past make us stronger.

732. If you can name your demon you can deal with it.

733. You cannot give away what you do not have.

734. If you don't put your job in jeopardy at least once a year it probably isn't worth it.

735. All things come to an end.

735. All things come to an end.

BUZZ WORDS

A

B

C

D

E

F

G

H

I

J

K

L

M

N

O

P

Q

R

S

T

U

V

W

X

Y

Z